AF573676

The Straw House

Retold by James Riordan

Illustrated by Trevor Dunton

Once upon a time
a little mouse saw a bag of straw.
'I will make a house out of straw,'
she said.

She put up the walls.

She put on the roof.

She put in the door.

'I like my straw house,' she said.
And she went in.

Just then a rabbit saw the house.

'I like your little house,' he said.

'Can I come in?'

'Yes, do,' said the mouse.

Then a cat saw the house.
'I like your little house,' she said.
'Can I come in?'
'Yes, do,' said the mouse and
the rabbit.

Then a little dog saw the house.
'I like your little house,' he said.
'Can I come in?'
'Yes, do,' said the mouse,
the rabbit and the cat.

Then a big wolf came to the house.
Can I come in?' he said.
No, no, no! You are too big,'
Said the mouse, the rabbit,
the cat and the dog.

The wolf was very cross.
'I don't like you and
I don't like your house,' he said.
So he blew and blew.

‘Stop, stop!’ said the mouse,
the rabbit, the cat and the dog.
‘The house will come down.’
But the wolf blew and blew.

The roof flew off.
The walls flew off.
And the door flew off.

'Now what can we do?'
said the rabbit, the cat and the dog.
'We can make a house out of bricks,'
said the mouse.
And that is what they did.